THE LATENT TALENT OF CONCEPTION

The Latent Talent of Conception
Copyright © 2017 Mindy Goorchenko
ISBN-10: 1542988314
ISBN-13: 978-1542988315

Cover design by Ana Grigoriu-Voicu

www.mindygoorchenko.com

THE LATENT TALENT OF CONCEPTION

BY

MINDY GOORCHENKO

Dedicated to Jane Kling

"Understand right now
 that all that you have seen
 has merely been
 a thought about yourself."

CONTENTS

Want-Spread...1
Nervous Geography..5
Bright Wheel..6
Soundforms...8
Body of Mind...12
Bowing at the Foot...14
Lumina..15
Flame of Souls..17
Menses..20
History of My Fall..22
Slouching Beast..23
Answer..24
The World of Dew...25
Empires...27
Awake...29
The Half-Life of Transformation.................................30
Bridging the Distance...32
Four Concentrations..33
Fugue..38
Hokku...41
Breaking the Covenant...45
Game Theory..47
Eulogy at Good's Death..50
Time's Crux..51

Want-spread

That's what they mean by the womb of time: the agony and despair of spreading bones, the hard girdle in which lie the outraged entrails of events.

William Faulkner

The dream woke up,
with all of its possessions.

It offered what was
final and prepared. After that,

what was once still
pressed at the edges.

It became real.
Desire dealt its blow, and

either the dream satisfied you
or didn't.

☐

(Strange sense that
what you didn't make
formed you—)

☐

Where the thought stepped in
wasn't how sides make a shape
less whole,

but how the line
aches to bend.

You were under
constrictive influences
beyond your control,

but you were also like a cup that
brimmed with the new drink.

When I brimmed
with the fullness
of a body,

and only what you
hadn't said
formed me—

(at least when you are brimming
you possess
the illusion of becoming
more filled)

how each circle
knows it is contained
yet eternal.

☐

This wasn't more real.
I brimmed with the
dream-body.

It shone with the
unconscious luster
I afforded it.

You became like
amber. Each hair was like
wheat.

☐

(Strange sense of
what wasn't—)

☐

What strikes me about reptiles
is not only the spine's length,
but how the heart
lines the ground.

☐

Can you ever feel
ploughed under?

As if the death energy in the universe
ganged up on you.
It delivered death
neatly, in a package,
with the word "hope"
stamped on it,

and your future seemed sealed
so you opened it—

☐

(Strange sense of
what wasn't—)

☐

I see I hadn't acquired the focus.
I was still overwhelmed
by the background of my life.

There must have been a trick—,
some flex involved,
which stated,

"this is not the danger
but the *prize*."

☐

(It's like communicating
old wishes.)

My ancient summoning:
Combine!
Combine!

(So that I'm through I must
trade places, enfold the
bright face of
no answers—)

☐

Though hard,
the edges of the diamond
symbolize the versatile—

☐

That's not what I meant.
The bones aren't spread.
They house the secrets—
dream-cups.

Strange sense of what wasn't,
brimmed—

Nervous Geography

The thing in the voice left
spoken sounds,
no simple animal—

Just a telling
made up
like a phrase,
met between
two openings.

This is basic exchange.
It rests in the lip,
the breathing,
each space
parted from me—

my simple current,
my loud, strange movement,
my wavering.

Bright Wheel

The frozen thing
(past)
still moves.
It doesn't need to ask.

Some bright face
motioned to the sleep

Grasp!
Label things!

And so I called it *wheel*
when I bled,
even how it stilled,

and either way
the earth
kept its tilt,
moved—

past the red planet on its right,
past the left hip of its maker in the sun,

until the whole view
fell backward.

And I was fresh
but this newness
seemed relative:

the planet still suffered
in the mad ecstasy
of pulse and breath,

and how is this reunion of the pores
with the aftermath
so different

from the slap of baseballs
fitting soft mitts,
under plum blossoms
tailored to a deep red?

The frozen thing
is the past.
Creation treads—

It is still unsatisfied.
It lingers with a twist,
carries with a turn,
a spin—

Soundforms

...because the limited always finds its limit in something, so that there must be no limit, if everything is always limited by something different from itself.

Aristotle's Physics

I.

Enough times however,
while the earth's green skin
swirled, an aura—

Form fought matter and
became sound. The first shape
let loose with a breath's force.

So the ear became attuned.
Outside that loud rest
heightened by the black stir,

the eye and ear made a pact
so that the thing could move.
It slipped into the clearing.

But the tongue interfered
while the mind caught up,
remembering each of Orion's belt stars,

Virgo's forked tongue
shooting off comets like
insults

steady yet
quite slow—

(how the will
in the first place
named then
hushed)

II.

That was the night
after your wife
gave birth:

I saw your feet for the first time,
I learned you would have done it at home,
and that you didn't name your son for almost
two years.

III.

Everyone around is

We can't see the differences
while being consoled.

(love to you is
jealous)

IV.

Orion's waist got cinched
with three loose stars like
buckle-holes—
doom caves.

The first wish
not too deep—
(a treat or a
small gift)
passed then blinked.

The second was a
woman's cave.
The blood swam and
the belt got stuck there.

When the last chose wisdom
a third eye entered,
and sat down where the
prong moved in.

V.

(even
desiring a person
is to desire
knowledge)

I wish to be
wise today—

a sphere or a
small atlas.

VI.

The bed dried up.
The dust on the bedframe told how
need wasn't safe,

and the broken parts
became holy
with the wanting.

You were living in a
fine place, where
emptiness was infinite:

this space

could easily have been the
same space as

this

and we were where the
emptiness could move.
So I left.

That was my excuse
for not having.

Body of Mind

In this body,
I often listen to the voice
where I once thought
time existed,
first of all,

and then my own voice,
which now rests,
questioning the seat of itself—
whether there *is* one
secondly.

I'm dying to be touched
for now.
There is a well in me,
some generic
fountain of inspiration.
I'm loyal and crazed.

I stand at the center
transforming your joy
into my body.
Touching you
represents something
I haven't figured out.
Watching you kiss
unsettles me.

My heart is punished.
This new place I am
startles me. I think
how can I find myself in you?

Then grasp
imaginary innuendoes,
as if to say

here—I've finally
found myself,

your voice
sending something
into me,
a blessing
or some other
equally unrealized
dream,

and I shoulder
this space
between boundaries,

the dream of our life
crept into my basket of hope.

Bowing at the Foot

The psychic that I'm always visiting
Is stupid, inauthentic, and a jerk.
High-pitched impressions from his hairy mouth
I always find impossible to hear
Until he says something that's so profound

I blow my thirty bucks and let him flirt,
Marauding incarnations he recalls,
Where he and I have spent entire lives
In bed or hanging from a wooden cross,
Always together, back-to-back, and nude.

While writing prayers for Americans
Paramahansa Yogananda
Compared the human spirit to a wave
And warned against delusions of oneself
Existing as the ocean in totality.

My guru's dead. Perhaps it is a ploy,
My naked trust one-sided and so blind
That he sees everything, while I avoid,
Observing spaces in our lives,
Protecting calendars from scrutiny—

Though anyone would be hard-pressed to name
The wave as something other than the sea.
It climbs and disappears within itself.
It houses everything within itself,
And while it changes, nothing is destroyed.

Lumina

This space and I—
blank patch of wall
braced with wood. I think

Bones. One-way
valves of veins.
Wire from the stereo face: stark
recurrence of a groove.

Beaming at my son's first
scream and squint.
Hollow tubes and destinations.
Bright beckon.
Sulcus.

While pregnant,
I faithfully fondled photographs:
the cloud and mist of ultrasound,
pages lit with liquid glowing Buddhas.

It didn't occur to me
for years
how black it was.

Dumb belief—
placing faith
in some dank
orifice.

Time. Progress. Blood's
swank stain. Slow heave. The dog's
pressing pant.

Reading the map
on my son's face,
how it swallows everything.

Disjointed reflections
of order and disorder. He spins.
I weave the tale for him.

Like time asks,
shall I circulate?—and
let him pass through me,

his wonderment that
probes with a threat,
loosens, lashes,

like water on a stiff stain.

Flame of Souls

Time swam through its miserable pool
of longing and despair,
past the frozen frame
of some last chance,
while the Breath of God couldn't find
anything to move—

It floated through the fourth dimensional field.
It played around the happening like some
celebratory event.

*

On our first date,
propped up against a chair in your
swank garage,

noting only how my legs
blessed your face and neck,
how the pyramid beneath my waist
filled your mouth
with strange jagged hope.

*

Though nothing here is fresh,
and there are too few words
to claim otherwise,
I would have left the vision
groping at the bed
(sacred blueprint),
planning my life
the way it had been.

Time swam through its violent pool
of waiting and despair,
sweating the last round like some
ancient champion.

It sunk beneath the covers of the bed.
It bled behind the pillows and the
useless threads of comfort:

the ease of sex,
the latent talent of conception,
the discovery and consumption of fruit—

You tell me
that my unborn son will be depressed
if I keep listening to Joni Mitchell.

*

When we had spent time enough
wondering about past lives,
some sort of abandonment issue
flitting through the karmic cycle
we had come to find this time around—

I'm through with trusting parallels
(as if we made the right choice)

I'm pregnant for the second time.
I think I'm in love with introductions.

*

Strange, isn't it,
that when you're here
I become this absent.

I was so in love
I tried to make myself
transparent,

like the matter I invaded
made the gray
less clear—

Out of the first attempt
what can I say comes?

There is only longing.
Endpoints give themselves up,
though you say they wouldn't care.

Where we once were
is where we were—
I only fight to regain
the ancient leverage.

Menses

My willing delay,
our heady denial of time-frames or management
melded at the third on-ramp.

The getting-there I understood.
Receiving your message—
like stealing that Sylvia Plath book
last checked out in 1988—

Not this sure
fading of the ink
on the upslope.

All the letters now are about
rain or sun, or barometer readings,
flayed tips of the unparted—
the snap of rain
while trying to form
symbiosis, allowing
each second to possess
familiar charm,
the digital face
as much a part of me
as ash-trays or postcards.

Two days later all that's left
are two trucks
parked next to one another
in an empty lot,
their broad noses,
glazed eyes, and
bumper grins.
I cared so finally.

That sentiment and hilarity
of inanimate rescue.
The static alarm.

History of My Fall

Rating death. Measure of less and great.
Breath pleases life in the body. Brazen.
Braised. Calling some thing that. *Life*.
Project, erase. Laughter at the trick of longing.
Rating union: Measure of time and space.
Trick of words: Othering.

Potential creating means. Itself acrostic
Intricate circulating. Measure of fate and decree.
Nocturne establishes sleeping: Dreams
Seeking black basins: Pressing the piece.
Keeper of the pinprick, reflex, delta wave.
Tools and tricks of the exchange: Death.
Sex. Separation. Sleep center. Passion of differences.

Response, elevation: Variables of the trade.
Rating trust: Measure of sameness and difference.
Elfin, snake-like. Missile-like, mushroomed.
Cranial. Crazed. The crazed prayer of pain.
Teased and textual. Training the body.
Interpreting suave electrical impulses:
Always one thought favoring. Cast out.
Never a gift. Naked. Always history.

Slouching Beast

Like you've been managing this life outside of yours
Think of the word "wife" (tragic pull outside the body)
Where I hide behind the breath.

It's almost 12:30 in the morning.
We act like there's nothing more to say
And I don't care about it.

The sprinklers pick this strange time to start.
I wonder if the baby monitor's working.
I don't hear cries yet wait for them,

Love pulsing through a thick cloud.
It forms a slight tinge on our faces.
We both smile,

Bending ourselves
While the truth presses down,
Though you're hurting and I'm hurting.

Answer

(The delicate question of asking—)
when what was sought for so long
holds me here now like vice,

and still not brave enough to speak,
I welcome each portion,
delegating inquiries
beyond the first life—

and wonder,
quite seriously,
if what you are now
slips beyond my reach—

plunging through that vague sense of godhood
in your innocence,

that cloaks you
just barely,

semi-nude—
waxing and waning through truth
like moonlight

The World of Dew

There was a time to feel these things:
how to start
keeping something;
how to make
feeling.

Afterward,
the way you nudged my chin out of the way
so you could kiss my neck
once—

while the wind
kept blowing flowers
into little cups:
want-clusters,
each stabbed in turn
by an indifferent insect.

Some days like this,
I spend entire hours
underneath death,

wondering how we started
pressing life through
thin paper images.

Grasped-at metaphors
waggle their flagrant clichés,
as I attempt to recreate
that previous fear of waking.

It is not enough to test
each loose end,
finding how the road splits.

Each path has not been
clear-cut.

There's only one way
to break apart
and this is it.

This is not the first time
I made someone forget
where they came from.

Her hair's so silky,
it's no wonder that you can't
stay harsh.

But I miss
your blank pages
wrapped like a book
you'd let me keep
opening up.

Empires

All I discovered that year,
while draping limp, orange cheese over the plate
was I existed,

gliding over concrete
amid the dog shit's simmering stench,
plucking White Bunny's hair from my pepperoni.

My soul heaves to the beat
of Bus Song, or Spider Song, plaguing my thoracic cavity
as efficient as a nervous system.

Give up the ghost, it speaks.
Here is spacetime's lull. The blind tilts from the rule.
Tugged on, tangled strands determine its position in space.

I've curled up in the blanket's dream,
the impressive excuses: Divine authorization of apathy,
desires, fantasies, and their ultimate meaninglessness,

the paradox of uncertainty. June bugs blind
whack against the glass. Bleed from my heart.
I've patched this space a thousand times.

A child straddles my thigh. I try to act engaged,
flitting momentarily to some vague hypothesis: the egg,
for instance, which formed him,

occupied my body from its birth,
blueprint sketched in the ovaries of grandmothers before me,
invoking, I suppose, some sense of divine awe,

and discard this idea of an outside.
While he pokes at my eye, it is actually I
who am prodding—

Awake

A thing cannot exist
before the most basic
minute form
traces possibility

the paint being
two dimensions
pressed by solids

each stroke possessing
infinite shape and contrast.

Blended
you are the motion of all tones
pressed abstract

where bright
lengthens into space
color shaping form
pressed.

Granted,
you performed
honorably.

At dawn
your light
and shadow
brim.

The Half-Life of Transformation

What is the perfect solution
while we're at it?
Where can we now go,
painless and selfless?

Dying to remember,
I realize more
when you're here,
leaving me
to flail and wander.

Everything becomes validated.
How can you do this?
Deliberating selflessness
this time around!
You rogue!
You waxing crescent!

I write to you every morning now,
finding myself
in these worthless things.

Traveling back to that time and place,
I try to remember
what was said.

I can even remember the poems
which drove my life.
But I don't mind.

Deadened by my own words,
I thought about singing to you
many times.

I had a life
dying to greet you,

yet kept itself
sorry and desperate.

Blanket my past with an ideal.
Shoulder my future with some obligation.
Anything but this.

Bridging the Distance

Though it's hard to rest outside of you,
the way a boulder on the surface of the earth
might crave union—

I remember pulling up their white bodies,
feeling depressed as to how to gently place them back down
upon the centipedes and other insects.

A stone had a sense of self even,
some still awareness
teasing each tiny piece of itself
into movement.

And while it suffers underneath
the quick burden of a single moment,
one point between the present and the past—

Behind the transparent gate
of what came to be named
"eternal,"
I'm trying to sleep
in the same bed.

Where were you
when you were here?
And if I tried to move you,
how could I ever
lift you anywhere?

Four Concentrations

I. Painful Concentration

What I wanted when I
moved in
wasn't like movement—

where there must have been
something more to it,
some final sense,

not leveled by the
first welcome.

But my body feels
trained for this.
I think my shadow
must become
more pointed,
more deliberate,
like a shark's fin,
or a tooth—

A wick
floats calmly
in its own body,
like the most
undue person—

where the flame
tucks itself in,

and you wanted it
to sigh beneath
the weight of itself,

shrug its
hypothetical shoulders
and renounce
all sense of self—

II. Wicked Concentration

A well-hung heaven tries to cradle us,
though we are stable on that
long flight south of ourselves—

(There's no salvation for us wishers)

So I fancy you
shuffling through the photographs,
drilling past the loose folds of the dress
and the long hair.

(Coupled with the idea
is it any wonder—)

What I've wished most
must land.

The sky is so
pleasingly pervasive.
It swings past the house,
and we liked being
this surrounded.

But it's a myth—

The myth of infidelity!

(The married ones
don't sin,
I'm fully convinced
at this point)

III. Righteous Concentration

Get back down here though—
it's this idea of movement.

You wanted so dear to know that
flesh couldn't move
without spirit,

and so I thought
you must be right,
since you wouldn't.

But what
possibly
could she make sacred?

Outside,
a spider darts beneath the edge,
not moving in the light's shadow.

You have found
the safety of the shade,
where the light's
more discernible.

The umbrella bobs
to and fro,
causing the sky to
change place.

IV. *Pure Concentration*

I am hurting,
the way a word hurts
when it's hung onto.

I sat wondering
how 59% of the moon's surface
could be seen

until my mind
dipped—
unevenness!

(We seem to forget
the shape of things)

But to lose a whole life there—

(Even the windows moved,
so it was that much more
difficult to see)

So I blessed the
small crevice,
less thought-out,
unseen—

(it is not
the idea of you
I love)

Fugue

I live behind your
messianic touch,
sorting through the various
saving graces:

Time and its
gratuitous destruction,
clinging to its
vague hold
on rebirth,

While you express
confounded
*Without time and space
how bored we are!*
(deliberating selflessness
this time around)

I realize I've forgiven you
only because
I've wanted something,
some storm in you
I probably made up.

Stiff-necked,
uncircumcised,
claiming the identity
of *blazer, forger*,

While you chuckle
I have always been depressed,
a Greek myth
freed and bound
over and over,

braiding God's face
like stems.

Maybe loosened,
I have garnered many kin—
transparent
legions of your tome.
Even you have said

Feign
indifference.
Licked,
chastised—
endure.

And so
I must know,
just as all men
arose once
as one man,

What space
became shared
between us,

What spirit
descended upon
the blank verse,
the harsh praise,

Proffered,
as a prophet
obligates the future,

Dusk to dawn,
damned and deadened.

You keep yourself
well-hidden,
as if you became
precious suddenly,

and pull my nightgown down
so I don't get on you.

Hokku

I.

I write
while trying to equate
failures in my life.

(that's not right.)

I write
while trying to press sight
into momentary blindness,
that lifted then
dropped,
like the hair of the
girl on the swings.

So I swear that
in this light,
where I have finally found you,
the grey becoming
so alive
that the sky seems fake
where it clears—

though this causes
such a catch in you,
everything was most high,
according to the Buddhists,
even this strange birth,
holy as a
seasonal reference—

fuyuzare:
the bareness of winter
popularized,
out of a need to feel
commonly barren—

II.

While servicing the basement of your soul
I decided that I
wouldn't go there.

So we've joined each other
once again,
as if fifteen lifetimes
weren't enough.

While laying above you on the couch
I explain to your higher self
how nature is contingent—

namely,
how the soul
makes its plan.

(deciding the exact moment
each tree decided to become
permanently bent)

In the most
seemingly unfavorable
circumstances,

while we wade
through the years

and I make some claim like

*autumn is the most
beautiful type of death*

what I really mean is

please be here

III.

I asked
what role would you grant?
Where is the strange tale
that guides my life?

Some time ago
(you had said)
there were two paths.
One shone and
one hid.
To this day,
I can't decide
which was which.

And so I have to ask,
though you have forsworn
each past life,

while nature
suffers and passes—

I write
while trying to press sight
into this,

as if you needed this strange
linked verse—

(liking how writing
is so automatic,
and that
just the same
hurting you)

Breaking the Covenant

                    Color of the past
and of the future, of the movie screen
at rest and of blank paper

I could have.

                      Robert Pinsky

Sitting alone,
I piece your clothes together,
finding the right way to deck
this cold space in my mind.

Aside from the mockingbird's
obvious symbolism,
I have painted
a generic picture,
having my night
shattered
by its bold reply.

The miracle has
supposedly
waited for me
all these years.

Intellectually,
I have conquered the body,
attempting to worship
the unseen face
behind its solid edge.

What do you have
I ask
that I don't know.
Do you think I cannot
pick this up
where I left off?
There is only
one poem
in my life.
I will write it
until I die.

Your response
in my still voice
tricks me like a snare.
I barely notice it,
until I realize that
it isn't there,
and you have not said
anything,

and fight your holiness
like sin—
trapped
like a saint
in stained glass,
bound and tangled
in your worn, black raiment.

Game Theory

Training ourselves to speak
without speaking.

Learning how
to break each other.

The painfully slow process
of extricating ourselves—

Enumerating losses.
Ill-begotten, blessed,

Cradling the ashes
like an infant.

Married to a time and space
you have loudly beckoned,
breaking the crash,

And I answer you
the only way
that I know how,

Pouring graces.
Convinced that,

If I empty long enough,
somehow

You will
hold me up.

Having spent
most of my life
being tried on,

Lost quickly,
overpowered, or
overcome,

What's the crime?
Believing
like anyone

That two bodies
can become one,

A crescent
caving in on itself.

Impossible clawing,
like trying to talk,
wearing

the cellular matrix
we divide
inherently,

Clutching
our chests
to our palms.

Whether fear or love
speeds us up,
the dream

Flashes.
The mind
disrobes.

This pervasive
whatever-it-is
how can you control?

Eulogy at Good's Death

Aware the body
this familiar
will receive

the brave gleam
steering from redress

the dull whir
of the ampersand
conjoining two businesses

amid the bearers
and the tellers
of the dream,

my gorgeous mute—
bright-faced dawn,
grave dusk of
soundlessness,
stark eve—

Bring an end.
Bring a no-end,
but *bring*.

Time's Crux

Prior to this present
(does this really make sense?)
we brought our own
deluded dreams
to the infinite.
Time's purpose
seemed to show itself
in small increments,
instant by instant,
claiming nothing but itself
each moment,
being flooded by the
wash of change.

When the reason
for this distance
seemed imminent,
we punctuated
each instance
with our full awareness,
climbing seconds like
small pools,
moving backwards to the
previous domain,
and found the place
where we had always been,
perfectly pristine,
shining in a
timeless grace,
unmoved—

Enjoy a preview of *The Discovery & Consumption of Fruit*, Mindy Goorchenko's next collection of poetry, due to be released in 2018.

Hildegard of Bingen

The light visited—
as if the first spark
was not aware.

It sunk beneath the crib,
the small pillow.

A body quivered
then reached for it.

The fingers played with it.

A tiny hand
tried to grasp it—

but only ten fingernails
shone
like bright crescents.

She would only tell this later,
after it had happened
more than once—

how the light
was like a shadow,
hidden as it
commonly was.

"It was like the star's
first pinprick.
The barn seemed to tremble—
this I will attest.
(At that age,
who would ever guess?)

The newborn calf
looked the same as
I remembered.
I felt like Jesus—
forget the reasons.
The nurse seemed
quite upset."

But how could light
bear the darkness?
She searched the
main source,
chasing some
bright shadow.

"You could have
made space
for the other half.
But you went on
training what
naturally followed,
as anybody would
in the face of
such blackness."

A shadow's just a shadow
where the space gets hidden
like she was,
some place between
God's home and God—
We supposed
some brave spark
got trapped between
the first thought
and the form.

"I had lived
five years
in the light's shadow.
I was never that big.
I think I just
got swallowed."

A holy arm
shuffles through the
loose gems in the drawer.

"You've heard how
Lucifer was thrilled.
But this is incorrect.
The jewels of his cape
popped back into the earth,
flailing as he was. Here.
Put the lapis underneath your tongue.
Place the jasper in your ear.
He won't come near,
the sight makes him
so undone.

"I don't know how
anyone these days
gets ill."

(A wink from
St. Disibod)

As if the first spark
was not aware.

The water kept reflecting it.
The fire burned itself thin.
Earth and air kept
wearing on.

"One must recover
from the idea of shadows.
I have never lived in blackness."

ACKNOWLEDGEMENTS

Grateful acknowledgement is made to the following publications in which some of these poems first appeared: "Nervous Geography" & "Soundforms," *Beloit Poetry Journal,* Fall 1997; "Want-spread," ¡*ZamBomba!*, 2003.

I wish to express my gratitude especially to Mike Filce, a faithful friend and reader who has proffered encouragement and feedback for more than two decades; Brenda Hillman for her enthusiasm and for permitting me to audit her class many years ago; St. Mary's College of California for bringing such poets as Robert Pinsky and Jorie Graham into earshot for readings in the late 90s, their voices still powerfully resonating in my memory; Robert Hass, whose *The Essential Haiku: Versions of Basho, Buson, & Issa* influenced pieces in this collection; Jeremy Pataky for an honorable mention in the 2017 Alaska Statewide Poetry Contest; and the comradery and friendship of many dear friends and loved ones who have particularly encouraged me as a writer, including Teeb Al-Samarrai, Noor Al-Samarrai, Melissa Bechand, Tiffany Borges, Debbie Corette, Joel Davidson, Alicia Don, Janna Kegley, Anastasia Kenney, Jane Kling, Joseph Koss, Vera Little, Regi McClain, Jeremy McKenzie, Connie Moretti, Mike Mulloy, Hanni Poli, Lauri Taylor, Debbie Voetberg, and Sarah Wald; my team members at the MDC who walk alongside in the difficult work; my parents and in-laws Bianca and Robert Splinter, Mike and Debbie Richardson, Tony and Vicki Goorchenko, and Jennifer Goorchenko; and lastly and most significantly, my husband Alexander who unconditionally loves and supports our family.

Our children have shared my time and attention with many endeavors; their excitement is always palpable and infectious, for which I am grateful. My hope for them is that they express themselves at the truest level and continue to grace this world with love and beauty.

Made in the USA
San Bernardino, CA
31 August 2017